UNDER THE STARRY NIGHT

HANNAH MARIAM

Writer's
Pocket

First published by Writer's Pocket in 2022

email: publish@writerspocket.com

ISBN-13: 978-93-6083-774-7

www.writerspocket.com

DEDICATION

Dedicating this book to all those with whom I have traversed paths under the starry night who influenced me,
helping me inhale the vibrant colors the night sky had to offer me, which led to the genesis of new or awakening of hidden feelings inside me.

Though poetry has impacted me,
I would not be capable enough to have found the right words to compose it without all of the feelings I have ever felt.

Like the different phases of the moon, passing through cycles of growth and decline, life has allowed me to see through the cloudy sky, shining brighter and beautifully.

I owe it all to the inducement I've received from the people whom I'll always love.

FROM THE AUTHOR:

"for all the lost ones,
you're not alone."

"and here I am,
trying to make sense of it all—
falling, failing, and rediscovering.

*i bring forth all five stages to recovery
for you to experience, feel and
breakthrough again.*"

CONTENTS

My mind woke me up -

my heart was screaming,
That's when I knew it was time to write it all out.

AGONY

i have come to realize that I like the winter season

better, the silence speaks to me, it gives me comfort after
daylight, the warm fire soothes my soul
it's an awakening from what once was
to what will be. often,

I wonder what it's like to be as free
as the winter nights.

maybe my heart feels safer because the chilly winds hug my
soul and find a way to caress my blood,

a puzzle of emotions – my heart is tangled
between wanting to doze off into my world of relief
and fighting to stay wide-awake
and surrender to the feeling

"The dawn will light up your life and its brightness will
reach you in places you never knew existed."

promises of the new day
bring me hope,
they sing to me
the song of better days

i know now what they mean
when they say stay calm in spite of all the chaos
and be aware of all the art that lives in you,

i fall deeper into the reason for my existence,

      envisioning what my future holds,
      constant thoughts cloud my mind.

the ache, the longing
of what could have been my world
is now a mere wish,

it pains to see my world fall apart,
to experience agony at the start,

   thinking a lot about what could've been and what is,

   How long before I eventually have to pick a side?

*"there is a world ahead of the hurt and the agony,
open your heart to all the experiences to be truly free."*

"Sleep comforts my mind and soothes my soul, it puts me
at ease. I will eventually come, I have to wake up soon
but for now, I am in my cocoon."

my bones ache, my heart is heavy,
how does one let go, how can one be happy?

let's begin again, start all over,
collect my pieces, break free of the misery,

i feel broken and numb,
i don't want to succumb,
there's no peace,
there's no escape from this glum

when the world gets

too much to bear,

i put on my

protective layer.

the lights are out, and so are the stars,
oh, what a lovely night!
chilly winds get under my skin

i looked up to the sky and shed a few tears

how do I feel the cold so much in such divine darkness?

The night has just begun, and I'm already drowned by the
words left unspoken, the bonds that are broken.

On such nights, I feel alone. it's almost as if the world has gone
quiet, and

not a soul is awake, i breathe heavily into the night, trying to
take in fresh air and release all my worries.

*"speak and get your message across, keeping the words
in will do you no good, speak into the night."*

How lovely you look tonight!
the heavens shines upon me with all its glory,
Will you keep my secrets safe?
I feel like letting my heart speak today.

the lights are out, the wind is gushing.
as i look up to the heavens to blink away my tears, I think to
myself,

Does my help come from up above or deep within?

several clots remain, words spoken —

they chose to pierce even more mercilessly until i weep into the
lonely nights. it was as though bloomed roses

chose to bear more thorns to tire my superfluous worries.
words once used to satisfy my heart, but now like the seasonal
leaves;
they drift apart, and leave nothing but emptiness.

i try to find hope in mundane life, but nothing helps,
everything just adds to hopelessness.

"speak gently, speak words of joy and hope."

my reflection in the mirror looks the same
and so does this places,

       but there is an invisible darkness,
         and a broken vase

i wonder if the change is external
or is it me who isn't the same?
i don't know the origin of this pain

      Is this what they call the agony of change?

       my cocoon is broken,
       around me there is no one,
       I ask myself, who am i?
       the darkness still covers the sky

i reach out to the lord of heavens for help,
save me from myself.

i'm in my head, there is no escape, it's a dark place
it feels like I'm in a maze,

running to a place unknown, i reach nowhere
time stands still, there's nothing there

How does one find the will to speak?

words don't do justice to the feelings inside
which is why

they never make it to the mouth

hiding my feelings only makes them stronger,
i'm unable to let them escape
or find an escape for myself,

I wonder why I do this to myself.

screaming away the pain,
goes in vain.
nothing helps anymore,
Nothing feels the same.

scattered thoughts
all around my brain.
they've got no place,
they need to escape.

screaming with agony into the sky,
        o the one who made the universe!

Can you hear me?

the pain is too real,
 too much to bear

How can I heal when I keep falling down?

down on my knees, i surrender to life,
It hasn't been easy, not a pleasant ride.

breathe in, breathe out, i tell myself again

i have to be whole again,
        i have to find myself again,

I'm hopeful yet hopeless at the same time.

I know I have the strength to get back up after every fall,

but I'm also tired of falling again and again.

I wait and wait for help from above.

my confessions are safe with my room,
i choose silence over regret,
i choose silence over overthinking,

my emotions are
like an unsolved rubik's cube,
when I don't speak,

silence is the only comfort i know,
silence speaks to me,
i can hear the whispers of the wind,
the sound of it fills up the empty house,

the city pauses but i can hear the hustle,

i become voiceless
in the presence of my realities,

yet I cannot speak.
i don't know if i choose silence
or if it has engulfed me
and i'm unable to speak,
either way,
i know it is better this way,

hearing my agony and pain
might make it too real for me to cope

*"Silence is the moment between now and after,
it is the moment of truth."*

it has always been a famous fight,

        the one between darkness and light.
        desires, feelings, all wrapped up in vain,
        misery being the only gain,

like the future out of reach,
the beginnings one can't see,

        do you know what it's like to mourn something
        even before it ends?

questioning, doubting,
such my nature has become,
forming an appetite,
only satisfied with pity, which is my only true friend.

how do i go on,
when I question and doubt everything?
what do i cope up with,
when nothing makes sense?

"I don't know why I can never feel like I belong."

Agony feels like a long way from home,
black are my steps on the winter snow,

      a blood-orange sun has set again,
      marking the end of another day.
      there is bitterness to this routine
      the sinking sun is my confidante,

the summer birds fly away

      summertime sadness has just begun,
      all the colors of the sky fade,
      i mourn this ending every day,

      Why must the sun go away?

it leaves me in darkness and with memories that i can't escape,
      i'm left

      holding my breath

yet again,
the orange sky blazing like fire,

the winds of change ache my heart,
they bring me sorrow and despair,

a tear rolls down my eyes
and my vision becomes blurry,

oh the agony!

the weight of sadness on my shoulder,
numbness in my eyes,
hopeful for light and revelation,

but all i get is darkness in disguise, agony creeps in and stays
much longer, it brings out my hidden wounds, the cold wind
burns my face

and stiffens my skin, and with a warm sigh and a breathless
gasp,

I bid summer goodbye.

LOSS

25

the love has suddenly disappeared,

no one responds when i call your name,
the blue skies have turned gray,
the water has made a grave exit,

thoughts tear me every second of the day,
my heart weeps,

my soul longs to look at one glimpse of your face.
not knowing where,

i looked for you everywhere,

i sobbed out loud, out of despair,
i called out the angels to help me look,

they spread to every nook,

but returned only to heal my soul

help me,
i cannot feel whole, i cannot cope,

my heart was with you when you left me.

where did you go?
are you trying to hide?
is this some test to prove my love?

i want to become whole again,
i ache to be with you,

why must i go through this pain,
why must all my love go in vain?

like the gardens ache for rain,
my heart aches to see you again.

"when you lose a loved one, you lose a part of yourself
that never comes back."

the thought of you shakes me to the core,

there is weight on my chest,
the heavy absence of happiness

has left me in despair,
the only reason i feel like i'm alive
is the heaving of my chest,

left with an open wound,
healing is   far away.

the idea of what could've been drives me to tears,
sewing myself up to become whole again

but i'm hollow and lost,
searching every face to find you again,
endless grief takes over, and the fact
that you are now a distant memory

— this is the art of being empty.

i'm trying my best to cope up with it,
but i keep failing

but even as i fail,
I still hope that I might see you again.

"Off you go into the land of strangers - nostalgic
memories will keep me company."

people come and go, the memories remain,
forever is just a word, but it can last as long as us.

time has taken a grave turn,

      i don't know who have i become,
      i see my reflection in the mirror,

      Who is this person? I don't remember.

the pain of change stings my heart
but it was necessary to become such,
the wind whispers in my ear,
its words are cold, it makes me shiver.

    for even a caterpillar changes into a butterfly,
    we must get out of our cocoons and fly,
    embrace the transformation my inner self cries
    as i wander between my different selves

reminiscence,
i've been thinking about this word of late,
Is it related to time? or

is it about how I have changed?
isn't it strange?
i never realized when it all began,

i never thought i could lose myself,
like forgotten books on an old bookshelf,
you think you can pick them anytime,
but they crumble in your hands,

How do I go back to being myself again?

I have come to realize that our existence is temporary in more than one sense.
it is divided into hundreds and thousands of smaller phases of our life.

We are never a complete version of ourselves..
We exist differently, with different people, in different places, and at different times.

Like time, we keep changing. like time, there's no way back to past selves.

i felt hollow inside, yet there was a constant pain,
i took a deep look within and found sadness,
my soul strained,
there were also the broken pieces of my heart
that i had picked,

How can emptiness and sadness coexist?

it's a contradictory feeling; of feeling sad yet empty.
I wonder if the pain emerges from the hollowness
if the emptiness is a result of the pain.
maybe, the latter.
maybe,

The pain overpowers and engulfs everything else.
maybe,
it doesn't leave room for anything other than itself.
I wonder why it's so difficult to store any happiness.

i dream of happiness,
Sometimes you are a part of my happy dreams.

i glance at my past versions,

there's
sadness in their eyes, their voices break
when they speak

but these broken voices give my voice
the clarity it needs.
they tell me not to feel sorry for them,
for i'm a product
of their collective strength.

i keep going on, moving forward,
in the hopes that i will become whole again one day

I'm a culmination of all my past selves,
and you're a culmination of all your past selves.
Instead of feeling weak as a person, think of yourself as a
phoenix who rises from the ashes each time
it is burned.
every time it dies, a little part of it dies forever.
There are always some ashes left after rebirth.
like we feel a piece of us
missing after every hardship we overcome, after every loss we
bear. but like with every rebirth, the phoenix gets stronger, we
become stronger after every spiritual rebirth too.

my losses through my life include
loss of innocence,
childhood,
friends,
family,
home,
and love;

all the losses were painful,

all the losses left me heartbroken,

but the one that left me truly lost was my loss of self.

i'm still finding myself,
i'm still rebuilding,
but i don't know where to look,
in which cranny or which nook

i wait

for my old self to come find me,
i wait
for all my losses to somehow fill,
i wait,
in the emptiness inside and around me.

i thought i would wait forever,
that there will be no end to it
but to my surprise,
it turned out

it was all worth it

i finally see a sliver of hope,

a rainbow appears in the sky,
laughter has replaced my cries.
hope filled me up

and I bid the darkness goodbye.

i think of all the *Loss* I have suffered in life
i remember how i strived
to keep it all together,
to keep the dead ones
alive,

everything and everyone i lost
left a darkness in its
empty lot,
i felt forced to fill up this darkness,

i had to come up with a device,

i want to arise from this pit,
i want to live,

i want to breathe the fresh air outside,
and feel on my skin the sunlight,

i take out my stored away paints,
i draw the sun and clouds,
i pour bright blue at the bottom of the page,
i take a dive,

i couldn't believe i was swimming among fish,
with coral reefs at the bottom of the ocean,
it was all real inside,

i closed my eyes and took a deep breath,

i inhaled both water and air,
i opened my eyes
and found myself back in my room,
shocked and surprised.

maybe i haven't lost anything,
maybe it is all still within reach,

i smiled with the realization,
i peeked within myself
to find everything i had lost,
waiting for me inside.

REDISCOVER

45

after a long time of feeling empty,
I decided to take a look inside.

i found a lot of beauty
made out of love that i was ready to give,

i wondered where had it come from,
i hadn't thought about love in a long time,

but i realized this was what i was made of,
just pure love, from a source divine.

i discovered i was made of love,
and it surprised me

       for i had lived in a cruel world,
       for a long time, i suffered
because i was looking for it outside myself,

it's like when
you search for signs of divine all around the world,
but don't consider yourself

       as a marvelous creation and a sign of God

just as my existence is a sign of divine.
i now know that i have a source of infinite divine love

within me, i'm letting it fill myself and pour out,

I'm now surrounded with love.

i thought i was a delicate flower
that dies when it's plucked,

i was afraid i wouldn't be good enough
to be placed in a vase,

but it was only when my feet hit the ground
that i learned my truth
,
I stood firm and tall and grounded.
i'm no longer afraid,
i know i cannot be crushed or rejected,

I will bloom forever.

i have learned that we are never as weak
as we believe,
i have learned that beauty in humans is very different
than that in material objects,

all beautiful objects are delicate
but all beautiful humans are strong.

*"there are components of beauty we don't talk about;
they include strength, courage, and will"*

does anything change

between December 31st and January 1st?

why do we celebrate
when the clock strikes midnight?

What do we celebrate?

different phases of my life
have brought me different perspectives
and to different places on New Year's;

i have celebrated it with friends
without sparing a single thought,

i have meticulously planned it with lovers
to reignite love,

i once watched a Christmas movie
to celebrate it with my family.

but on the New Year's eve tonight,

i'm separated from everyone
for various reasons,

i was dreading to be alone,
but it gave me the peaceful moment
to think for once.

between the two moments
before the date completely changes,

there's hope,
a hope to let go
and a hope to start anew.

no matter how many difficult moments
we faced in the past year

and no matter how many difficult decisions
await us in the coming times,

we celebrate a shared moment of hope
for all of humanity.

I don't think there's any celebration as beautiful as
New Year's, all religions and all cultures celebrate it as one, the
joyful screams of
"Happy New Year"

        are for strangers and loved ones alike.

losing the one we love
> can be one of the most painful experience
>> yet,

blessings can be found in this loss
for one's soul.

it's better to lose it entirely,
than to live with half of what you want,

a half love can never make you whole,
it doesn't matter how

much love you think you can give,
needing it back is out of our control,

> love and misery can never come hand in hand,
>> we only agree to it
>> so our hearts are consoled
>> but the truth remains

that we want and need it all,
if not,

it can feel empty
despite having someone to hold.

if they cannot love you as passionately as you love them, you won't be able to keep

the spark of love going for long; love needs equilibrium, an inequality in love leads to feelings of

ungratefulness or emptiness; it should feel full, so much so that you choke on it with happy tears in your

eyes; don't settle unless you find love like that; until you find it, heal yourself with self-love.

when it was over between us,

all my love faded away.

for a long time afterwards
as i grieved for your love,

i never realized that i was grieving for myself,
not you.

it wasn't only the love for myself that i had lost,
It was also the compassion and empathy.

i thought i feared to love again
but it was as if all the love inside me had withdrawn.
the realization was difficult,
i wanted to find a culprit

but it shouldn't have affected me so much,

I know it is true.
it was a long road on which i found myself,
I was as full of love as when

you had left.
i embraced myself
and felt alive,

everywhere i looked after that embrace,
only love filled my view

Sometimes, we love so deeply that we begin to see the world
from our beloved's eyes. when they leave, it hurts

so much more as we stop seeing ourselves as worthy of love,
but it shouldn't happen this way.

growing apart from someone shouldn't be about our worth as
a person. in fact;

 it can be a new opportunity to find our changed self from a
lost love.

we talk about getting hope
from seeing the sun;
the warmth, the brightness,
and the yellow surely helps.

but i find the moon more resilient and strong,
hanging so close as if hanging by a thread.

yet maintaining a distance
and moving at its own pace,

passing over rivers, forests,
and alps.

in the darkness,
it gets by with whatever it can salvage,

sometimes as a crescent,
sometimes as a giant balloon in the sky.

to me, moon is the real bringer of hope,
a message of sympathy and understanding that is truly
heartfelt.

The sun is strong.

The sun stands tall and big in its place, always holding
its ground, but it is the moon that knows

how to keep moving
and to go through different stages, silently and resiliently. it becomes

thin as a sickle every month, and then fills up to become whole
again, all while moving, never stopping. it disappears to take a
break, it

knows when it needs rest,

but it knows that there's no such thing as giving up.

i remember all the times
i felt loved

by my mum through her unwavering support,

by my dad in the little ways he took care of me,

by my friends during our endless conversations.

love has many forms and languages,
my goal is to find them all.

We often doubt our place in people's lives when they

don't confess their love to us blatantly. but
in everyday life, there are so many moments when we

experience the love of our beloved ones. we will never

feel alone if we simply open our minds and hearts to
receive love spoken in different languages.

maybe life isn't as difficult
as our impatience makes it look,

slowing down
and taking time
can do wonders and miracles,

we are not supposed to be happy
the very next moment
of feeling sad,

we don't have to try to
relax all the time
to never feel worrisome.

life's difficulties aren't supposed
to magically disappear or
disappear completely,

life is lived in seasons,

just like the seasons of a year,

each season of sadness ends,

when a season of happiness arrives
and each season of happiness ends,

when another sorrow arrives,
you might like one more than the other,

but each ends after sometime,
we just have to be patient.

"rediscovering life is an art that needs to be practiced at
all times."

to be impatient is to be human
but faith can be bigger than confusion.

you don't have to understand it fully
to make use of all its solutions.

let it be handled by who you bow to
the Lord who is one.

we are imperfect and weak
after all, mere humans.

let go and let God in you,
he will bring it all to the perfect resolution.

search for the lesson that needs to be learned every time you get hurt, it will help you understand God's plan for yourself and help you reach what is meant for you sooner, we delay our blessings when we refuse to learn our lessons from the hardships,

God brings the sun up in the sky
after every dark night,
let Him do the same with your life.

have you ever planted a seed?

if you haven't
let me tell you how it grows,

you bury a seed all alone under the earth,
you mark the spot
when you plant it

and then you wait,

as you wait,
you also give the seed a little bit of water,

you wait some more.

then one day,

after you have gotten used to waiting,
and don't even consciously wait for the seed to grow,

you see it sprouted,
its very small at this stage,

and very delicate
but it's there

above the ground, alive and proud.

our efforts in our lives are not very different
than planting seeds; we plant ideas and water them regularly so
that they grow;
for a successful life, we have to get used to the idea of caring for
the seed
 and have to stop thinking about snatching its fruits; the plant
will grow, the fruits will drop when ripe,

the flowers will bloom; all in their due time.

the moon inspires me,
appearing strong and beautiful in all its phases,

it always shows up,
no matter if the light is little or too much.

you appear like the moon too,
always strong, overcoming
wave after wave,

even when you are not around,
your beauty and resilience
remains untouched.

i hope you cherish what you have become,
beautiful, yet bold and brave,

always adding light to darkness
with energy & warmth

i hope you get the courage
to *Rediscover* your life, your self, and your happiness,

i hope you rediscover the joy in strife
like the pleasure of cooking late on a Christmas night,

like bathing under the sun on cool summer days,

hearing laughter of children and crashing waves,

i hope you feel excited to go on new adventures
to find the tallest mountains or the earth's center,

i wish you the courage to find happiness and more,

to discover what's hiding behind the closed doors,

for life isn't over yet and there's more out there,
waiting for you to experience another breath of fresh air.

they say you cannot get back the lost time
but I believe in rediscovering everything that was once mine.

for time moves in circles,
it will bring back what was lost,

don't stop your feet from moving,
keep your fingers crossed.

CHERISH

the secret to a happy life is simple

it doesn't lie in deciphering complex symbols,

it lies in moment to moment,
in accepting life,
ripple by ripple.

free yourself of the
material things, don't count the
pennies and nickels,

remember that sad moments
 are temporary
and you will be able to rekindle,
happiness in

every moment
and revive the patience.

cherish your life as it comes,
make an effort to see the light in darkness.

make an effort to accept that light,

and you will find
all the happiness,
even beyond your expectations.

I hope you choose to cherish your life.

we search for many things in our lives,

the perfect partners and the right careers

but if there's any search in life,
it is only our ability to adhere

to who we are and how we accept it
without any unnecessary care.

without the self love and self care,
not much makes sense

in the absence of the acceptance of one's self,

it cannot matter whatever is present,

in contrast, where there is self acceptance
it becomes easy to feel content.

82

in present times, we measure our worth on superficial, worldly
factors;
but in truth, our earnings, our homes, or our degrees don't
determine our worth;

The only measure of worth comes from self-love, we should
only try to love ourselves more and more every day;

*and we should only try to reach a point in life where we truly,
unconditionally love ourselves.*

the most cherishing moment of your life...

will be the one when you realize
why it all happened,
why you went through what you went through.

in that moment,
it will all make sense

for once, in a small moment,
you will understand

why was there ever any suspense?

but don't wait for that moment
because

it wouldn't be what you imagine,

while you will cherish it when it comes,
you cannot keep your heart closed in
defense of

disappointments and sadness,
for you will also miss cherishing any happiness.

as goes an old saying,

"no pain, no gain,"

as kids, we find it cliched

but truth can be found
in hearing it again.

seeds rupture to grow,
humans can be the same,

pain accompanies all change,

can you tell a caterpillar dissolves in itself,
before a butterfly, it became.

cherishing the pain that comes with growth
can be one of the most challenging things to cherish in life, but
we constantly bear so much pain that we never realize exists;
our cells die and are reborn all the time, even a mother goes
through immense pain when her child is born

but as long as we breathe,
even if with difficulty,
we can find something to cherish.

the breath that keeps us alive also brings us many reasons to be happy.

Are you ready?

to get to the end
and find the secrets
that have been forever hidden?

do you imagine how you will feel
when you find out

it's not the end,
it is where it all begins,

all over again, as if nothing has changed

but it all feels different,
Nothing is the same.

when it all begins again,
you will learn to cherish everything

the change we go through, the many rebirths we experience
during our lives are moments that needs
to be cherished,
to be celebrated,
our bravery doesn't only show in the face we put in front of
the world,

but the face we are left with when nobody is around.

*take the difficulties as opportunities and you will always
live in a happy moment.*

i think of the perception of happiness
of our happiness being limited to us,

can we be happy for someone who isn't ourselves?
wouldn't this world be a better place

if we cherished happiness from every source,
if our perceptions weren't so coarse?

if we only looked for joy a bit more,
we might find it a flowing river

from which anyone can pour
or a vast sea with endless shores,

open to all, and then some,
for as long as the eyes can scan the coast.

yes,

life isn't fair, and it can be especially difficult to feel happy for others when things aren't going right for us,

but we can make the joy ours by genuinely feeling good for those around us;
i promise you,
 there is something that can bring us joy at all times, even if it isn't meant for us;

moreover,
once you begin cherishing others' happiness,

happiness will find its way to you in other ways too.

the universe tells us to wait,

yet we become impatient,
it tells us everything will be okay,

yet we feel agitated.

in this impatience and frustration,

we miss those vital signs,
we ignore His guidance
and wish for things to resolve quicker.

but in this foolishness,
we miss out on our growth,

we isolate ourselves from the world
and end up feeling alone.

hard work and prayer
goes hand in hand,

combining them together
helps us truly achieve our goals.

we are impatient creatures,
but there's virtue in patience;

in our impatience to listen to the loud blow, we ignore God's
little whispers that can be equally as valuable and bring our
hearts contentment and happiness;

cherish the wait, listen to the silence, and
find harmony in existing with patience.

chasing after things
only brings confusion,

it only makes them messy

instead, sit back
and let things unfold,

for them to reveal clarity.

confusion only entangles you more

life, when messy,
can be uneasy,

*live in the moment
and you will have happiness only.*

making the most out of life doesn't mean chasing things and
people constantly,

 it doesn't mean you should try to get everything done quickly
and altogether,

instead, it's about living in the moment and letting things be,
the only time you need to be worried about is that in present,

don't waste it by living a messy and confused life, not anymore;

*start living every moment and every moment will only
bring you reasons to cherish life.*

let it be a reminder

to let your heart loose,
to feel fuller and happier
and to not reduce

the moments of happiness
or hit snooze
when it comes knocking down
as truth.

let it be a reminder

to cherish the sky's blue
and enjoy the nights
as they unfold to you,

let your lungs breathe free,
exhale as much air as you drew,

that's all it takes to shift perspective
to make your life feel anew.

"don't be scared to cherish life."

moving on can be difficult,
cherishing the lessons can be challenging

but it is the only way
to heal the heart.

if you truly want
to stop dwelling in darkness
and pull through,

you will need the light for the new start.

cherish the confusion before you cherish the clarity,
take your pain and turn it into art.

let the sun shine on you and the air surround you,
let your thoughts be engulfed and washed.

Cherish moving on...

       moving on without cherishing
      will only cause you to step back later,

      the puzzle in your life won't complete
       without the missing parts.

gather all sources of joy and contentment,
spiritual growth and healing has no other cost.

get over the fear of emptiness
or loneliness,

      the longer you hold onto sadness,
      the longer it will take to depart.

you can only recover from the hurt you have endured, when
you begin to replace it little by little with happiness;

sometimes, we hold onto hurt because we are scared of what
might take its place, it could be worse, right?
not necessarily;

*find the smallest of joys and see how they fill your heart and
make it warm; allow happiness to recover your soul...*

RECOVER

the sun and the moon

move about in their own paths,
yet in tune.

on days, the sun hides behind the clouds

and on days, it shines bright,
like in June.

but what goes on on earth never affects it,
instead it causes
storms in dunes.

moon always maintains its course
even if we don't see it,

nothing makes it hide
in a cocoon.

we can all learn many things from these stars,
trust me, healing can be easier in communes

like the journeys of the sun and the moon,
our journeys will also have days and nights, clouds and storms,
and a change in seasons;
but just as the sun and moon stay on their path no matter
what, we are meant to do the same;

after all, we are also made up of stars..

do you remember the night
we treasured each other?

we embraced under the moonlight.

there was a full moon in the sky
but to me, you shone brightly.

the sky above us was nightly purple,
The sand in our toes was white.

you told me you enjoyed glancing at my countenance
and gazing into my eyes.

all your dreams and wishes
to air, we chanted and recited.

it was the night your adoration healed me
and ended all my days of plight.

believe in the healing power of love;

but don't limit the love in your life;

love can come from friends and family and even strangers;

absorb it in all the forms it comes into your life and let it
breathe in a new life into you.

you were swift to show me kindness
when I was hurt

but you couldn't offer it to yourself,

could you?

we all have so much kindness filled inside us
and we know spreading it makes it expand.

but we waver to show it to ourselves
and face a dilemma in getting it through.

there's no damage in being kind to self,
it's not wrong,

it's no taboo.

let's take an oath to pat our own backs
and help ourselves recover and renew.

while accepting other's love and kindness can heal us, we can also heal ourselves with our own love and kindness;

self love is the greatest love there is and a path to recovery from all of the worldly ailments.

sometimes in sadness,
there is concealed
what we need at that moment to heal.

instead of wanting delight and excitement,

if we only feel what we are meant to feel.

we can get over the unpleasantries
and not lose our zeal.

remember, life moves in circles,

bliss takes over sorrow upon
the turns of the wheel.

don't alter or prevent the life's motion,
with time, it will all be revealed.

let your tears flow
if they must,
they will soon turn into ecstasy squeals.

nobody wants to hear to just do it, to just move ahead, but sometimes it can be the only way towards recovery.

"In life, sometimes the only way to get what you want is through something you don't want."

if you have ever lost a loved one,

then trust me, you will find love once again,

you may feel like it's not possible
but all that you have lost, you will regain.

believe in it and it will happen for you,
There's no reason for hope to be slain.

the sun will shine in the sky once more,
Nobody said it will always rain.

*get some fresh spring flowers for your life's vase
set the table, pop open that champagne.*

our fears can hold us back in many aspects of life;

one of these aspects is love but there's no reason to hold back love and recover with it;

let your heart heal by the new love;

let it make you happy.

nights can be the most agonizing time,

all those with broken hearts know
it to be true,

it's when the whole world is silent

that the heart aches for what it seeks

to all of you,

I say,
peek at the glow beyond your windows,
allow yourself to see how the world continues,
moving on, moving ahead, never ceasing,

you can also reach and get through.
nights may be challenging but they do always

come to an end,

the sun still comes out,
you know it to be true.
"There is no rainbow without the rain."

don't spend your nights crying over losing the day,
instead,

prepare for the next day to come so you can make the most of
it.

do you think about

connecting the strings of someone's heart,

of gently cupping their face,

holding their hand
and wandering under the moonlight
or
	just pausing in a silent embrace.

	love can make you see unexplored colors in the sky,

it can make you feel blessed,

it can make you see the identical things
with a unique perspective
where everything fits
in its perfect place.

don't say no to love if you encounter it again
and don't be afraid
to see what new love can produce,

let the fate reveal what it has in store for you,

I promise you,
goodness awaits.

finding new love can make one scared;
but new love can also heal, don't be afraid of new love,

it can be the one you truly deserved.

after rain comes the rainbow,
making the sky glow

with colors

blue, violet, and in between,
as a spectacular show.

but rainbows only follow rain,
on their own, they don't come out,

similarly,

healing cannot occur without pain,
crops only grow after months of plow.

there is beauty in the hurdles,
after rupture and repair,
you grow.

all the pain can have meaning
but only if you allow.

recovery and healing only follow pain;
you cannot expect growth if you are not ready to accept the
difficult days,

learn from them, and move on in life.

I wonder where the notion of closure first came from,

How did it become so ingrained in our minds?

How did we become so anxious for the last words?

Why did peace become so hard to find?

I believe to move on from our pasts,
all things that remind us of that past
needs to be left behind,

let's not hold accountable those who broke us

and let's overlook those who weren't kind.

our recovery has always been in our hands,
we can have it as we choose to design,

our lives, our hearts, and our stories,
Let's break free of closure and its confines.

we don't have to have a last conversation,
we don't need to listen to an apology,

we can choose to make our lives better despite not getting
closure,

We can recover without anyone's kindness.

we can choose to be kind to ourselves, after all, there isn't a better
closure than finding a happy new beginning.

do you trust yourself,
or do you trust fate?

either way,
there's no need to be afraid.

you will reach what is yours
or it will find you, even if delayed.

don't let your fears,

'cause your trust in God to fade

or let you believe
that you couldn't have escaped

what you never liked

and what caused you to dismay

from what you loved
and didn't want to unmake.

your destiny lies in your own hands
or in the hands of God,

either way, it's in the hands where
your wishes will never be betrayed.

sometimes we cause hurdles in our recovery by not trusting the
process,
not trusting that our destiny contains as much healing as we
need and wish for;

 i'm sure you must have experienced this too, but with trust,
we can change that,
you can change that;

we can heal if only we can trust that we deserve to recover, so
believe that, and see let the miracles happen!

most of us are guilty

of undermining the power of words,

we tend to take lightly
all that's said and heard.

but words can heal us
as if nothing had ever occurred

and help us *Recover* from pain,
to make us, once again, undeterred.

kindness and compassion
and empathy and concern,

though are valued as actions

also need to be translated as words.

let this journey through words help you,
let these words cure your world.

As someone who picked up this book, I believe you
already have faith in the power of words;

I want to reinstate this faith deeper inside of you, and
introduce you to their healing powers.

Never underestimate the power of kind words you can
speak to yourself.

ONLY FOR

your eyes....

Hey, you!

I'm glad you picked up this book, and even more glad that you
have come to its end.

You may have witnessed that I was there,
                              by your side, through the entire journey.

We began with Agony,
                              a position where nothing made sense

Accepting the heart filled with anguish,
we moved on to,

                    Loss,
Where we discovered to tolerate the losses that
surfaced in our lives

            and uncover something unknown in them.

From loss, we moved on to Rediscovering,

learning with each verse that what we lost,
                              We can find it again.

then, we learned to

Cherish;

the new and the old,
once we cherished what we had and what we have, it

helped us Recover

from our agony.

Each verse was a step; each chapter,

a phase of life.

I hope you shared your journey with me,
from agony and loss to rediscovering and cherishing,
and finally,

Recovering.

I hope it helped you assemble the
fragments of your shattered heart and
arranged them together,

I also hope that it allowed you to fill in

the missing pieces
that you couldn't find.

Every time, life has damaged me, I have encountered
reassurance in words.

Reading words from others and
writing some of my own are both adventures

that are close to my heart.

while reading helps me feel apprehended;
writing inspires me to heal,

some people find it illogical
that I recover through writing,

that words recede my ache and the
discomfort of those around me,

despite

one cannot truly comprehend the power of words until one
makes use of them for their rescue.
I firmly believe that reading or listening to the right words at the
right time can aid one in recuperation.

I desire reading my words to have enabled you to understand your emotions,

mended you, and permitted you to recover.

ABOUT THE AUTHOR

Hannah has been reading poetry since her youth, but after encountering the reality of life, she began authoring it too.

Divided into her five main stages: agony, loss, rediscover, cherish and recover;
This compilation of poems means a lot to her.

Hannah is intensely in adoration with what she poured forth in these blank pages wrapping every corner describing and making sense of each of her feelings throughout; saying:
"This collection is all for you to read and feel the aura of every verse I've penned down. Now that I've got somebody to communicate it with,
Let me walk through the beautiful and imperfect days with you."

Writer's Pocket

Writer's Pocket is a publication house established in 2016. We began with the aim of providing a better publishing platform for aspiring writers and budding poets.

The publishing industry in India (and around the world, to a great extent) is always something of a mystery even to the writers themselves. We are working on making publishing more accessible to everyone.

So far, we have helped over 3,000 writers turn their dreams into reality by publishing the books and continue to do so. By doing so, we also provide some of the best content by Indian writers to the readers.

Want to read more books? Scan this QR code with your smartphone and check out all our books on Amazon.

www.ingramcontent.com/pod-product-compliance
Lightning Source LLC
LaVergne TN
LVHW042153190726
843493LV00006B/1656